SLA GUIDELINES

Designs for All Reasons

Creating the Environment for the Primary School Library

Michael Dewe
and Sally Duncan

Series Editor: Geoff Dubber

School Library Association

Acknowledgements

This book is an update of the SLA Guideline *Ideas and Designs* by Michael Dewe, published in 2008.

We are grateful to Alan J. Clark of Designing Libraries for writing the profile of Michael, who died shortly after this book was first published.

Thanks to Geoff Dubber, former SLA Publications Co-ordinator, and Sally Duncan, former Assistant Director of the SLA, who guided the revision of the original edition.

Published by

School Library Association
1 Pine Court, Kembrey Park
Swindon SN2 8AD

Tel: 01793 530166   Fax: 01793 481182
E-mail: info@sla.org.uk
Web: www.sla.org.uk

Registered Charity No: 313660
Charity Registered in Scotland No: SC039453

Printed by Holywell Press, Oxford

Cover image: Pixabay/Bru-nO

Contents

Introduction

An outstanding school library for today (and tomorrow)

'The school library should be exciting and welcoming and identifiably different from classrooms. As a multi-media interactive learning environment, it motivates pupils to explore resources for curriculum related work and their personal interests and stimulates creativity.'

—Primary School Library Guidelines, CILIP, 2015.

Creating an outstanding primary school library involves more than just planning, designing and constructing an attractive, stimulating and welcoming space for the school community. Whether a new build or a refurbishment, to create an outstanding facility, the school will need to take the opportunity to think about and review:

- The role of the library, as part of the school's drive to raise attainment for every pupil and support learning for the 21st century
- The range of materials it will house
- The services it will offer to the school community
- The way it will operate on a day-to-day basis and the person/people who will manage those tasks.
- The reasons why scarce resources and time *should* be put into a physical space and resources when money could be spent on buying devices for every pupil which can be loaded with content that might supply all of the pupils' information and reading needs. There are many reasons – too many to list them all here – but three important ones are:

  - A well thought out, well resourced, well managed library makes a huge statement to pupils, staff and parents about the high regard the school has for reading as the foundation of learning. Pupils, staff and parents will take their cue from that statement.

  - Taking real pleasure in reading – both fiction and information books – is underpinned by choice. Choosing to read or not read, choosing facts over fiction, choosing a comfortable or challenging read. Choice is harder on a tablet or other device. In a library you can see the whole cover, read the back cover, feel the thickness of the book, check the contents page or the index and see what is next to it on the shelf which might be more interesting. Devices are good if you know which book or author you want to read – they are not so good for browsing (in my experience).

  - A well-managed, well organised library can transform learning by opening up opportunities for self-directed research. It can develop skills for learning by becoming the learning space where pupils formulate questions, think about keywords and phrases, find information sources, take notes and present what they have found out in their own words. It can also alter the ways that teachers teach and encourage interclass cooperative teaching strategies.

Library planning and design is a demanding task and adequate preparation and active involvement are crucial. This Guideline provides a range of ideas about:

- The background thinking to the planning process itself
- The importance of consultation with everyone involved – and how they can make their contribution
- The creative process that results in an exciting and stimulating new library for everyone to enjoy
- Guidance on practical matters
- Case studies
- Resources to assist schools in the planning process, such as details of books, furniture and equipment suppliers, organisations and websites.

The library in context

All primary schools need a number of learning resource areas – a hall, perhaps a drama studio, PE area and, of course, an effective and clearly demarcated school library. All these different spaces feature under the 'learning resources area' umbrella term.

Building Bulletin 103 – Area Guidelines for Mainstream Schools defines learning resource areas as 'timetabled space used for learning and therapy' and they 'should include… at least one library or learning resource centre (LRC)'. The primary school library should be one of the most important learning spaces in school. It should be a place accessible to all, staff and children and maybe parents as well. A place for formal as well as informal learning and for leisure and quiet relaxation. We would hope and expect that 'formal or whole class teaching' would sometimes take place in the library, for example during the research activities associated with project work, when the children are using a wide range of resources to locate and gather information. This means that the ideal primary school library would be big enough to accommodate a whole class for learning and active engagement with those resources. Effective, better designed and inspirational primary school libraries will also include areas that can be used for a variety of purposes: browsing; personal study; reading; perhaps quiet activities such as playing board games; guided reading; and storytelling.

Determining the role of the library, its relationship to other learning resource areas, as well as to classroom spaces will be an important part of the planning and design process.

Primary schools will often be faced with one of a number of planning scenarios. They could be:

- planning a library for a new school
- planning a library for an existing school that has somehow managed without one or has been struggling to make best use of the school's entrance hall or a busy corridor. This might be a new build or the conversion of an existing space within the school building or grounds
- refurbishing an existing library, i.e. redecoration and the replacement of furniture, shelving and equipment
- remodelling an existing space, possibly involving structural alterations. This is normally accompanied by refurbishment
- planning the extension of an existing space. This will usually involve both the refurbishment and remodelling of the original accommodation to create a unified whole.

Whatever the precise circumstances, the aim will be to produce an attractive and exciting library that will enhance teaching and learning and provide enjoyment and fulfilment to everyone in school. In a rapidly changing educational and technological environment the planning and design process that is suggested can only provide a framework for individual projects that may not always reflect an ideal situation. For example, the school may already be faced with a predetermined location and space allocation for the library.

Six steps to success

Where to start?

Planning and designing a primary school library may seem daunting to busy people in school. Where to start is the question that everyone will ask.

It may be helpful to break the process down into six straightforward and logical steps.

1. **Preplanning**: Asking questions, assessing need and coming to preliminary decisions.

2. **Planning**: Putting ideas and plans into writing – the architect's brief for the library or, in the case of a straightforward refurbishment, for example, the brief for the library furniture supplier.

3. **Design**: The formulation of and agreement to the design solution.

4. **Construction**: Plans on paper take on real form – much to everyone's interest and excitement! – watching the new build/alterations take place.

5. **Moving in:** Turning chaos into calm and order! The unpacking, the positioning and repositioning – pulling it all together before opening.

6. **Evaluation**: If necessary putting things right: deciding whether the library works as expected and finding out if everyone is pleased with the result.

Working to this clear sequence will help ensure an excellent planning, design and completion process resulting in the creation of an appealing library fit for purpose. It cannot be emphasised too much, however, **that the more time and effort given to the preplanning, planning and design stages the better the end result.**

Pre-planning: starting at the beginning

Here are 10 actions and issues to get you started.

1. Choose your leader

Some of the first decisions to be made concern people. For example:

- who is going to head up the project for the school? Will it be the head teacher, or perhaps the literacy or library coordinator?
- what can he or she do by way of preparation in order to successfully lead and organise the planning and design process?
- how will the school involve other people in consultation? After all, the new library will belong to the whole school not simply to the key decision makers.

2. Create a Working Party

A good starting point would be to set up a small group or working party – consisting of the head teacher or one of the senior staff who will lead the group, a governor (preferably the one with a library or literacy interest and responsibility), the teacher who has overall responsibility for the library, any member of the support staff who runs the library on a day-to-day basis, any interested parents, probably from the PTA, and of course, pupil representatives.

This group will discuss and formulate a design brief, discuss the proposed design with the architect or designer (if either is involved), keep a watch over the progress of the project and ultimately consider and plan how the school will celebrate the completion of the project.

Initially their job will involve:

- discovering the resources and information that will help the school understand the process and the kind of contribution that all the different stakeholders can make
- gathering and reading information and useful publications and examining case studies
- finding out about professional and other organisations that can help
- possibly visiting trade exhibitions
- visiting interesting and exciting new school libraries and talking to staff and children working in them
- browsing websites – see Appendix 1
- becoming familiar with architects' or designers' drawings, symbols and scales.

All of these activities will have a long term benefit as well as helping with the immediate project. Developing a knowledge and understanding of library design and space planning will be useful for the evaluation and maintenance of the finished accommodation into the future.

3. Ask searching questions

Answering the following questions can be a useful process in the pre-planning stage and help make the whole process a little easer:

- **Where** could the library be located?
- **Do** we actually need more than one library – one for infants and another for the juniors?
- **How** big could it be?
- **What** would we like it to contain?
- **How** can it be arranged to best advantage?
- **Who** will be responsible for the library and its management? Where will they work?

These are of course important questions – but we also need to consider more fundamental issues, for example:

- How do we expect the library to support teaching and learning and reading for pleasure across the school? How do we envisage using the library to maximise its impact on pupil attainment?
- Who will be using the library, now and in the future?
- What are and will be the library and information needs of these users?

We can only answer these questions when various kinds of information have been acquired and analysed in the pre-planning stage, which profiles the existing library (if there is one), its use, and the school community.

In other words, effective planning builds on an understanding of the existing situation in the school, its library and local community – and also takes into account the school's vision and passion for its forthcoming new library. There is no point in spending many hours and a large amount of money unless there is going to be a real and measurable benefit to the school, its staff and pupils.

> **Be clear about what you want from the library, how you expect it to impact on reading attainment and how you will measure the impact in order to prove to stakeholders that you were right to spend the time, effort and budget on improving your library provision.**

4. Profile your existing library/provision

A useful way to evaluate an existing library is to compile a checklist of questions. Distribute your checklist of questions – as a simple questionnaire to all and everyone; teachers, support staff, governors, children, parents, etc. – to gather facts, figures and opinions about the strengths and weaknesses of the present accommodation.

The physical facility

The following questions provide a starting point, however, feel free to edit the questions and add ones which are more relevant to your situation.

The Physical Facility	Notes
Is it in the best location in the school? Can it be moved to a better location? Is it likely to be moved in the future?	
Do we like its layout? Can we make it better? What is fixed?	
Are we satisfied with the quality of the lighting and the amount of natural light?	
What impression is given by the current furniture and fittings? How safe are they? Are there enough?	
Is a counter needed? Is it in the right place? Where will the books be issued and returned?	
Is there enough space for teaching activities? Will there be whole class or group activities?	
Is there space for quiet study, browsing the books and/or reading?	
Is there enough working space for ICT and other technologies?	
Is there enough storage and admin space?	
Is there suitable heating and ventilation?	
Is there enough guiding on the shelves and space to display resources?	
Is there a noticeboard or display area for publicity or promotions?	
Do we like the entrance? Is it welcoming?	

Library use

An assessment of the existing library is better if not just based on an evaluation of its physical aspects, but put alongside information and statistics about library activities and use.

Consultation now and at later stages of the planning and design process is very important, particularly with pupils, as this helps to create a real sense of interest and ownership.

Think about types of library use noted on the checklist below.

Library Use	Notes
Membership – who uses the library? It may be more people than is obvious from looking at loan statistics.	
Loans – how many? Who borrows the most?	
Enquiries – are they recorded?	
Number and frequency of class visits – how do the classes utilise the library?	
Independent visits – how are these monitored and recorded?	
Library clubs and events	
When is the library open?	
Are there any timetabled information skills lessons?	
Do governors, parents, pre-school siblings use the library?	
Are there any pupil helpers – what are their views on how the library is used?	
Is there a library committee?	
Are there any library staff? How much time are they given? Are they paid extra for this important work?	

5. Profile the local community

Collecting and analysing information about your primary school, its community and any existing library provision, provides the basis on which to review the following:

- The library's purpose and policies
- Funding and management
- Staffing
- The range of learning resources to be provided
- Service provision
- Day-to-day practices and methods, such as buying and cataloguing resources and the use and training of pupil volunteers.

In putting together a profile for your school to be used for library planning, it is useful to consider the following factors about the local community and the way in which they might affect the new library and its use.

- The evolving local community:
  - are there any new housing developments? Are the existing houses being improved? Will the school be expected to accommodate increased numbers of new pupils?
  - transport links and how pupils get to school – do the majority live locally or are they travelling in from outlying areas with fewer facilities?
  - local facilities for children, including access to public/community libraries and the availability of local bookshops.
- The pupil population: numbers, age groups, social and ethnic make-up and whether these are changing.
- It is also useful to have a picture of how many pupils have homes without many or any books in them. These pupils will need greater help when choosing books to read from the library and, if there are a large number, how will this service be provided?

Also add to your thinking:

- School governance and structure – the number of teachers, support staff, parents and governors. How will the library be used to support these members of the community?
- The school curriculum and teaching methods now and in the next few years. Is the school looking to move towards a more project based or creative curriculum?
- School policies and its Improvement/Development Plan. How will the library support the development of the school and the learning taking place?
- External support, for example, from your local schools library service, the public library, the archives service, and local museum.
- The educational and technological changes that are taking place in the wider world, such as the greater emphasis on informal and personalised learning in schools and the ever increasing use of IT to support all aspects of education.

New or enhanced premises really do provide an opportunity for change, improvement and development and a chance to determine the implications that these might have for the proposed new library accommodation. Some of these pre-planning issues for review are outlined briefly below.

6. Consider the Library's Purpose

Consider the following. Is your library or will it be:

- a whole school resource, open to everyone – pupils, teachers, non-teaching staff, parents, governors and, in certain circumstances, the wider community?
- a means of promoting reading, visual and computer literacy?
- a place for study, learning, teaching (particularly of information skills), and for presentations and events?
- a way of promoting personal development and cultural awareness in pupils?
- a focus for Internet activity?
- somewhere that supports the non-taught curriculum, for example: the school ethos and staff development?

7. Consider Policies and Procedures

It can be useful to consider some key whole school decisions:

- What funds will be available for the new or refurbished library and for maintaining its upkeep and physical maintenance and development in the future?
- How will the new library be staffed? Will you include the use of pupils and volunteers and if so how will they be supervised?
- Opening hours – is the library to be open before and after school and at lunchtime? It will be much more effective if you can arrange this.
- What materials can usefully be kept in the classrooms? Which ones are better organised and managed in the library and which ones will you borrow from your local School Library Service?
- Which computerised library management system (LMS) will you use for cataloguing resources and how this will be implemented and maintained?
- How will you ensure the library is inclusive? How will access for children with special needs be organised and what facilities will they need?
- Will you need additional resources to bring the library up to a reasonable standard? The SLA recommends that the minimum number of items held in a library should be 10 per pupil. The active life of a resource item is about ten years, although in subjects such as science, technology and geography, and with paperback fiction, replacement will need to be made after about five years.
  The SLA recommends that the proportion of fiction to non-fiction in a primary school library is normally around 50–50.

8. Consider Resources and their Organisation

- What hardware will you need? Will you include an electronic whiteboard? A PC should run your library management system.

- How will resources be organised? The SLA recommends the use of the Dewey Decimal Classification Scheme for non-fiction and an alphabetical or genre sequence for fiction.

- Will the library offer some form of digital platform for school and home access?

- Displays are really important for encouraging reading – how will displays be managed and how much space will be devoted to them? Who will be responsible for this work?

9. Give thought to Provision

Looking at the layout of the school would it be better to have one large library or would several smaller zones be preferable? Whatever your decision, you will need to make sure the area can be used for a range of library and reading activities. Flexibility is essential.

Take into account that the library/libraries will need the following:

- Space for reading, viewing, listening and using computers by individuals and groups
- Access to IT, including a dedicated PC for accessing the library's catalogue and for issuing and returning resources
- Space to house fiction, non-fiction and reference books and magazines
- Audio-visual resources, such as DVDs, and printed formats, such as posters and charts
- Space to study and write notes
- Space to accommodate a whole class for formal teaching, usefully within sight of a SMART board
- Informal areas for browsing and reading
- A Storytelling/ storyreading area and perhaps a special chair
- Somewhere for displays that promote reading and highlight areas of stock
- Staff workspace/storage – this is often ignored or given scant attention. Make sure that you allocate a reasonable space. Having this space will make the job of the person who runs the library – either on a full time or part time basis – that much easier.
  The following items will be needed:
  - Shelving for resources and materials waiting to be processed
  - Work bench with lockable drawer(s)
  - A PC for cataloguing new acquisitions, plus printer
  - A filing cabinet
  - A book trolley or two
  - A telephone and internet connection
  - A locker for personal items.

Space will also be needed for:

- Equipment and supplies
- Library-centred events, e.g. book talks, book weeks and author and illustrator talks
- After-school clubs and related extended school activities.

10. Consider Size

Go for the largest space you can obtain. If the library is to be a central resource for everyone then it needs lots of space, hopefully with some potential for development in future years.

Ideally, the purpose, policies, spaces and activities proposed for the primary school library should determine its size. In practice, it is often the case that the size is dictated by what space is available in the school.

The SLA recommends that schools treat Building Bulletin 103 guidelines as a minimum:

> *at least one library or learning resource centre (LRC) with a total area of at least 9m2 plus 0.05m2 for every primary pupil place.*

Where space needs cannot be met immediately, consider how the proposed school library location and design might accommodate future expansion or extension of the library.

Think outside the box!

One of the 2017 SLA Inspiration Award primary schools solved their space and location problem by craning in a retired London Underground carriage and then converting it.

Several schools in the UK have bought and converted double decker buses... here are two – one the winner of the SLA School Library Design Award 2011 entries, and another of our 2017 Inspiration Award schools.

Rosendale Primary School, our inaugural winner of the SLA School Library Design Award in 2011.

Here is a picture of the upper deck which houses the fiction books.

Further details are available to read at
http://www.sla.org.uk/library-design-award-2011.php

New Milton Infant School, Hampshire have also bought and converted a bus into an eye-catching and exciting library.

Some schools, if they are fortunate, can allocate a spare classroom..

Charford First School has just developed a new library in a classroom space in a central location. (2017).

Some build a multi-purpose specialist room. As Wyndham Park Infant School Salisbury created in 2013. It was one of our finalists for the SLA School Library Design Award for that year.

See more details at http://www.sla.org.uk/wyndham-park-infant-school.php

Some go even further – Nansloe Academy at Helston in Cornwall, a thriving 3–11 primary school, not only has a well-established junior library, but also covered their central courtyard/atrium and created an inspiring 'story garden'. This greatly impressed the SLA judges in the 2013 Library Design Award competition, who awarded it a Special Commendation as it didn't quite meet all the criteria as a 'library'.

To read more about this exciting and innovative space take a look at

http://www.sla.org.uk/nansloe-story-garden.php

or see more pictures on the school's website at http://www.nansloe.com/our-library/

Planning

With the initial discussions and pre-planning complete, now is the time to commit ideas to paper and make a positive input into the designer's or architect's brief. A brief will also be useful if the whole project is being done 'in house' by school staff, as it will give everyone a clear idea of what needs to be done in order to achieve the vision you have for the library. The decisions you make now will set the tone of the library provision and its use for the next decade or more.

The following headings, some considered at the pre-planning stage, may be useful for preparing the brief.

- The pros and cons of the existing library (if there is one)
- The primary school library community
- The purpose and roles of the library
- The nature of the stock and the services and facilities that will be provided
- Day-to-day management
- Any library zones that may be needed – class and study area, quiet area etc.
- The particular qualities expected of the accommodation, e.g. flexibility, accessibility, and ambience
- Furniture and equipment requirements
- Costs.

When writing the brief include thoughts about the following issues:

The library space

Are you going to have one library space or several, or mixed activity areas?

a. Location

In many schools the location is pre-determined. If it isn't, then a central location is the best, bearing in mind the following important points:

- *that it meets the library space requirements*
- that it is not an awkward-shaped space that is difficult to utilize and supervise
- that it is located with a view to future expansion
- that it is located in a quiet part of the school
- that it has an external library sign
- that it has access for disabled pupils and adults.

Other factors to consider will be:

- Whether the library space or spaces be 'open' and 'visible' spaces or enclosed with four walls
- A location on the ground or perhaps an upper floor
- The library's relationship with other spaces – e.g. classrooms and computer facilities, if the latter are located separately

■ The importance of secure accommodation and security tagged equipment.

In short, the library location should provide adequate space and be readily identifiable and accessible to pupils and others, and relate well to other parts of the school, particularly the ICT area.

b. The library environment

In wanting to create a comfortable and appealing, quality library environment that is different from the classrooms, give thought to the kind of ambience that you wish to create.

Think about:

■ design features – will you have a 'themed' library with a jungle, castle or perhaps an undersea feel to it?

■ colour – will you want to change the theme in the future? If so, you may want to keep the walls, carpet and shelves a neutral colour and add accents or support the theme with posters, soft furnishings and accessories.

■ lighting – is there much natural light in the room? Do you need to maximise the available light by keeping everything in light bright colours that emphasise a sense of brightness?

■ flooring – is the room enclosed or does it form part of a 'corridor' where there is a lot of through traffic? If so, you may need to consider whether hard flooring might work better than carpet. It does mean that it might be noisier, however, and it will deter pupils from sitting on the floor to read a favourite book or magazine.

■ soft furnishings (curtains, blinds and upholstery) – they need to be washable and fire resistant as well as attractive.

■ display facilities – you will need both wall display for posters and pupils' work and shelves or tables that can be used to display books and other resources.

Good heating and ventilation must also be provided. Ventilation is especially important in a space where you may have a large gathering of people and a number of computers may be in use.

Space and equipment for the display and decoration of the library will also help create a varied and stimulating ambience, although it is important that posters, artefacts, and so on are changed regularly if you are to maintain a stimulating environment. Filling every possible space for the sake of it will only create a cluttered rather than an aesthetic appearance to the library.

c. Furniture

When selecting shelving and other furniture, look at a number of suppliers' catalogues for the range, materials and precise sizes of items and to compare prices.

The School Library Association **recommends** that the maximum height for shelving units in a primary school library should be 1200mm with the length of individual standard shelves of 900mm although some maybe 800 or 600 mm in length to fit awkward room shapes. Depth is usually 190mm, 240mm or 290mm. Shelves are generally adjustable at 30mm intervals.

Other shelf depths are available and many companies will make up bespoke units for you.

Deciding on a standard length and depth for shelves will make them much more interchangeable. Deeper shelving is available but will usually only be required for larger reference and oversize books. It is generally good practice to shelve oversize books as near as possible to the main sequence.

It is always a good idea to buy shelving from a specialist library furniture supplier rather than from the DIY or domestic self-assembly warehouses.

Shelving

Capacity: per 900mm shelf:

- General fiction and non-fiction, 30–36 books
- Reference material, 18 books
- Picture books, 36–42 books
- Face-on display, 3–4 books.

It is better to overestimate the amount of shelving you will need to take into account the fact that it is better not to completely fill the shelves so it is easier to add new books and to return books that have been borrowed.

Shelves can be:

- Metal or wood or a mix of materials – the choice is yours
- Colour – metal shelving offers a range of the bland to bright colours and wooden shelving can be obtained in a variety of stains
- Wall mounted and/or freestanding shelving. Wall shelving, with perhaps some freestanding island shelves, leaves the central library space free for flexible use. However, a library designed with a large amount of window space will probably demand more centrally placed, freestanding shelving
- Shelves should be adjustable and should have supports along the back edge to stop the books falling through. Bay and shelf guiding is important as well as areas for face on display.

Other storage furniture

- Kinder boxes for picture books
- Storage for large books
- Paperback carousels
- Storage shelves or containers for audio-books, maps, posters, pamphlets, magazines
- Storage for stationery and other processing resources, such as labels, book coverings, repair materials.

Seating

As with tables, think about providing seats of different sizes, or adjustable seating, if the age range of the primary school warrants it.

- At tables for comfortable reading and study
- At computer terminals if you have decided to plan for fixed PCs instead of wi-fi laptops. The ICT layout might then make use of cluster, rank or horseshoe arrangements. Do

you need special ICT seating – swivel or static seating – seats with castors – and fabric or plastic chairs?

The tip again is to try them out before you buy and do make sure they are comfortable!

■ Informal seating – bean bags, soft seating such as sofas or arm chairs, stools and cushions

■ Height – suggested heights of seats are:

280mm (age 3-5)

320mm (age 5-7)

360mm (age 7-9)

390mm (age 9-13).

Tables

■ Height – suggested table heights are:

500mm (age 3-5)

550mm (age 5-7)

600mm (age 7-9)

650mm (age 9-13).

■ Shape – a choice of rectangular, square, circular, trapezoid, for example.

Display and other equipment

Depending on the types of material housed by the library, other equipment could include filing cabinets, storage boxes, display stands and wallboards.

IT

You will need a PC for issuing and returning books which can also be used for cataloguing new stock.

PCs for internet research can either be in the library or classroom, whichever works best for your school.

It may be useful to have another PC in the library with the library management software installed so that pupils can search for a subject or author, find out which resources are available in the library and what the Dewey number and location of the resources is.

Health and Safety concerns

Make sure that the design of the library takes into account recognized Health and Safety requirements and consultation on these matters is advisable for all new library plans, schemes and alterations. These issues will include:

- Shelving – stability and absence of sharp edges.

The SLA recommends that you purchase from an established supplier who will ensure that these matters have been taken into consideration. It is best to avoid 'home made' shelving unless you are absolutely sure that it will be of the best and safest quality.

- Ventilation, especially when there are large number of pupils and computers in the library
- Noise reduction
- Flame resistant soft furnishings
- Electrical safety
- Proper cable management
- Ergonomics of the furniture, particularly those for use with computers
- Mobile shelving units must have lockable castors
- Access for all.

The next part of the process involves producing the design drawings or plans. If you are going to buy shelving and furniture from a specialist library supplier they will usually offer to come and draw up the design for you. They can also offer invaluable advice on what their experience tells them will work in any given situation.

If you are just making minor changes to the layout and perhaps adding a few more shelves a sketch of the finished layout will be perfectly adequate

Before settling on the final design have a last think about the layout and consider the following:

- Shelving around walls and island shelving on castors make for a flexible central space for events and other occasions
- A minimum of 1000mm circulation space in front of and between shelving units. This is a health and safety requirement.
- A fire exit, if required, will affect layout, as will the positioning of radiators, electrical outlets, and windows.
- The space relationship of elements within the library should try to ensure a progression from noisy to more quiet areas and allow appropriate supervision of pupils.

Location

Maintaining a library service, perhaps in a temporary school location while refurbishment is taking place, is a challenge, unless building work can be accomplished when the school is closed. A library extension, whether it involves new build or taking over adjacent spaces, is likely to pose similar logistical problems, as well as dealing with dust and noise.

This stage of the project presents the head teacher and working group with the opportunity to:

- develop and finalize the floor plan for the library – (mind you it may look very different when dealing with real shelving units and furniture!);
- make decisions about shelving, furniture, soft furnishings and equipment, including ICT, and see to their ordering – it can be helpful to draw up a checklist of what is required,

not forgetting smaller items, like kick steps, carousels for some genres, and blinds or curtaining;

- order exciting new resources for the launch/opening of the library

- work out, if this is appropriate, how the move from the old to new accommodation will be organized. This may include moving items of furniture and equipment, as well as library stock;

- create project milestones for important events by backward planning from the proposed opening date.

This is the time to really involve the children in the finer points of building construction as part of their curriculum activities and to record all the various stages for the archive, that will of course be kept in the new library...

If the schedule has gone to plan then the laying of carpets, the installation of shelving, furniture and equipment, and the shelving and display of books and other formats should suffer little or any delay once the building of the library premises is completed. It is now, as planning has become reality, that last minute re-adjustments will be needed. Involve the children and parents in the move, the unpacking of books and resources. Let them help to shelve books, put up the posters, notices and mobiles and test the ICT. Give them the opportunity and excitement of turning an empty space into a wonderful library. This will be good PR for the school and raise the profile of the library and its role.

Of course take the opportunity to organise a grand opening ceremony for the school and perhaps the community. Invite a popular high profile children's author or illustrator as well as other VIPs and representatives from the building contractors, architects and others who have contributed so much to your new library. How about organising a library party and book event or week for the children to coincide with the opening?

Evaluation

Once the library is up and running and welcoming children and adults, it is easy to imagine that the project will have reached its natural end. But there will be loose ends to tie up, such as undelivered items of furniture and equipment, and stock that will need to be chased up. Some items of equipment may not function as they should and there will be a call on warranties. There may also, for example, be finishes to be completed, adjustments to lighting needed and minor repairs to be carried out.

As well as checking the physical and technical aspects of the library and remedying any faults, the librarian or library co-ordinator will want to assess whether the library is working in the way that was planned and to the satisfaction of all. While obvious matters can be remedied, and the initial novelty factor will raise great interest and better use, in the longer term the satisfaction of users can only be judged by encouraging comments and feedback both informally and formally from children and teachers at regular intervals. Make sure that you show that the library is responsive to suggestions and criticisms.

It is also important to assess the impact that the library is having on raising attainment across the school and thus demonstrating its continuing value and the need for lots of regular funding.

The SLA self-evaluation publication for primary schools, *Quality and Impact: Evaluating the Performance of your School Library* offers guidance on collecting evidence and appropriate actions for improving the school library. In this way planning goes back to the start of the six-stage process described earlier in this publication. It shows that improving and developing the library service is a constant managerial activity, not necessarily associated simply with acquiring new or better accommodation.

Maintenance

A new library looks a treat and the challenge is to keep it like that. Without constantly assessing the quality of the library environment, its cleanliness, orderliness, and dealing with problems of inadequate guiding, out-of-date posters, tatty notices, worn furniture, and equipment that is out of order, the appearance and reputation of the library suffers. Good housekeeping is essential; so too a budget allocation that ensures the maintenance as well as the ongoing development of the library accommodation.

Over time, as curriculum priorities change, the library will undoubtedly be asked to accommodate new formats, new equipment and offer new services – in other words respond to change both internal and external. By adding to, and perhaps rearranging the library layout, it is easy for the library to become cluttered and unappealing. This may reflect a genuine space problem, which might be alleviated to some extent by a systematic weeding of the stock, for example, or it might require a fundamental assessment of existing library service priorities and activities. It may, of course, provide the argument for new or extended library accommodation to be embarked upon.

Refurbishment

The planning and design process outlined earlier can also be used when dealing with a library refurbishment or other planning scenarios. With a refurbishment, the location and size of the library are known constraints, and both may be entirely satisfactory for present and future needs. Where this is not the case, it is questionable whether refurbishment – however much this may improve the look of the library – is entirely worthwhile. A better solution is likely to be a move to a more suitable location within the school that provides adequate space for the library. Depending upon local circumstances, this could involve new build or the acceptable conversion of redundant or underused areas elsewhere in the school building.

However, a refurbishment may also present opportunities to extend the school library (if this is necessary), in the existing and accessible location. This too can involve new build or taking over adjacent redundant space. Adding to the existing library area in this way may involve some building alterations and this may be a more complicated project than a straightforward refurbishment – if there is such a thing.

In summary, refurbishment for refurbishment's sake, if improved accessibility and more space are important issues, may not be the best solution and other options should be considered.

Who Can Help with a Building Project?

Many individuals and groups within the school community will have an input into the planning and design of the primary school library. Of particular help will be the staff of your local Schools Library Service (SLS). It may have its own series of booklets designed to guide schools in this and other areas of its work and activities. A list of schools library services in the UK is given in the latest edition of *Libraries and Information Services in the UK* (2015) and is available on the SLA website at http://www.sla.org.uk/schools-library-services-uk.php. Alternatively check the local authority website for details.

From outside the educational environment, the architect, builder and library furniture supplier transform the library design from an idea into a reality. The architect offers a design solution to the stated requirements of the primary school for its library, and the builder turns this solution into a visible reality of quality. The products from the shelving and furniture supplier make an important contribution to the use and ambience of the library. If required suppliers will also usually offer an interior design service as part of their tendering process, which will create an appropriate library layout for shelving, tables and seating, etc. Suppliers that particularly serve the needs of school libraries are listed in Appendix 1.

Visits to other school libraries provide a fund of useful ideas. The schools highlighted in the SLA Inspiration Award and the previous School Library Design Award can offer some real inspiration and examples of good practice at http://www.sla.org.uk/inspiration-award.php.

Case Study

Barton Hill Primary School
A time-critical library project

Margaret Pemberton
SLA Board member and school library consultant, previously manager of
Bristol Schools Library Service

Barton Hill Primary School (now designated Barton Hill Academy) was opened in September 2006 as part of a re-generation project in a disadvantaged area of Bristol. It was composed of pre-existing schools, but they were now located in a brand new building. At the time that the library project was undertaken the school consisted of 450 pupils across the Key Stages. Importantly, the school had been in special measures since 2012 and two (job-share) head teachers had been seconded from high performing schools to try and turn things around. The school was also in the process of working towards academisation, which it wanted to achieve by September 2014.

In November 2013 Bristol School Library Service was called in to assist Barton Hill Primary in setting up a new library. Whilst the building was fairly new and there was a designated room 'Library', it did not look as if it had ever been used for that purpose. At this time it was being used as a store-room and had walls of wooden storage shelving.

An initial meeting was held at the beginning of November, in order to set the following guidelines with the head teacher in charge of the project; the requirements of the school were discussed in detail:

- Timescale for the project
- Maximum number of days work allocated
- What the school wanted to achieve with this project
- Liaison staff at the school
- Balance of stock required
- Stock management
- Budget available
- Future Planning.

There were several issues, but the main highlight was that this was a time-critical project with the school wanting shelving to be ordered by Christmas. This was because of the usual lead-in times for the ordering, construction and delivery of the furniture and ideally they wanted to be up and running by the end of March 2014 at the latest.

To formalize the work plan it was agreed that a Service Level Agreement would be written and signed by the School Library Service (SLS) and School, so that there would be a full understanding of the roles required.

Library Design

The school staff were able to look at a variety of catalogues and websites belonging to the major library furniture suppliers. There were discussions about how to use the space and what types of shelving and other storage would be required and eventually we, the SLS and school staff, decided on the set of criteria that they wanted in order to create the right atmosphere for the library.

- Main shelving should be around the walls
- The top shelves should be forward facing displays
- Spinners and kinder boxes should be used as appropriate
- End unit displays should be considered
- Seating and rugs were discussed.

The first decision was to decide on the actual design of shelving and then the colourway that was wanted. This gave the dimensions that would have to be worked with in calculating the number of units, their height and also the number of shelves per unit. We contacted the short list of possible suppliers and asked for a site visit before the Christmas break. However none of the companies were able to offer this service within the requested timescale. This meant that an alternative method had to be agreed. Peters in Birmingham (http://peters.co.uk/) were happy to work with us to plan the space if we measured the space and

listed the shelving that we wanted to include in it. This was a daunting idea as the room was not 'square' and the old adage of 'measure twice, cut once' was something that was taken to heart.

I visited the school at the beginning of December and measured the space, starting with a basic sketch of the room. This enabled me to take into account the following:

- Doors
- Windows
- Corners where shelves meet
- Wall height available
- Position of plugs and sockets
- Internet connection
- Walk through lines
- Desk position
- Position of spinners and kinder boxes.

All of the information was given to Peters, together with the type of shelving that was required. This included, design, heights, single/double sided, end units. Their staff then produced plans to meet this specification.

Stock Audit

The book stock for the school was currently spread around the building in classrooms and even in storage boxes. Most of the stock was past the age where it would be satisfactory in a new library, although it was planned to sort through stock to see if there was any, notably fiction, which could still be used.

The school decided that it wanted to go with a split of 60% non-fiction and 40% fiction, which is becoming more unusual, but it was recognition of the poor state of the current non-fiction stock and the fact that a new curriculum was being implemented. It also included materials for the Foundation Stage, which had not been included before and now needed to be catered for. A calculation was made about the number of books that could be accommodated based on the likely shelving quantity. This sample looked like:

4 shelves per bay, 10 bays = 40 shelves maximum

18 shelves non – fiction

1080 @ 60 books per shelf

6 display shelves

16 shelves Fiction	640 @ 40 books per shelf
Paperback carousel	120
Picture books	150 @ 75 per kinder box

A meeting between SLS and school staff was then held to discuss the topic areas that needed to be covered and a list was made. The talks were in depth and a comprehensive list covering both KS1 and KS2 was agreed. There were also some additional subjects such as poetry, jokes and puzzles and recreational non-fiction added to the mix.

Stock Purchase

Two members of the school staff were delegated to work with SLS to make sure that all stock was purchased within the timescale and to the specification requested. There were two visits made to Peters in Birmingham; the first was on 15 January and the second on 30 January 2014. The timescale for delivery is usually 1-2 weeks, so there was plenty of time for the stock to arrive and be placed on the shelves. The boxes arrived in mid-February and were stored in the room until the shelves were fitted.

The purchasing was divided between the three of us, with one teacher taking the picture books, one starting on the non-fiction and I chose the fiction. Given that the non-fiction would take longer to assess and pick there was an agreement that help would be given in this area as other types were finished. The one thing that proved to be very important was to keep control of what had been purchased and the amount spent. There is a tendency for all book lovers to act like 'children in a sweet shop' when they visit a library supplier, so it is imperative that everyone knows what they are doing, that they have lists and keep a firm control over their spending.

It was agreed with Peters that they would fully process all of the stock. These included jackets, spine labels, bar coding and bibliographic records to be added to *Junior Librarian*. This meant

Fitting Out

Because the library space had been used as a storage area it was necessary to work with the site staff, as well as the teaching staff, in order to move these materials to other parts of the building. All of this had to be done by the beginning of February so that cleaning, painting and electrical work could be done while the room was empty. The fitting was booked for 24 February and it was agreed that I would spend the day at the school to supervise the fitting and answer any queries that the fitter might have had.

On the appointed day, the fitter arrived for 7.30 am and all of the materials were checked and unpacked. They were then sorted into the relevant piles. The actual construction was completed by 2.00 pm and this included two kinder boxes as well as all of the shelving. I would definitely recommend having the fitter because of the time saving, efficiency and skill that he brought to the job; it was quite amazing to see the level of competency. It was also useful to be able to ask questions such as 'how do we change the shelving to the "face forward sloping" mode?' and to be shown the process.

Whilst I was overseeing this process I had the time to complete a list of actions that still needed to be completed, they were:

- Check books against invoices
- Put books on shelves, in order
- Staff induction and use of LMS
- Put pupils on LMS
- Complete signage
- Print off subject indexes and a classification schedule
- Pupil induction
- Library policy
- Annual plan for next academic year
- Add other books in school to the LMS
- Classify any stock needing this
- Parent helpers.

The actions listed in italics were those that could be termed 'Phase two' of the project, whilst the others were actions necessary for the start-up of the library.

The first of these actions was started later that week, on 27 February and although it seems straightforward it was still time consuming. A lesson learnt was to unpack and check invoices one box at a time, otherwise you have to go searching for titles and this adds to the workload. The whole process of sorting the books took 3.5 days spread over a week, but finally the stock was ready for use.

Moving forward

As the project neared completion the school decided on a few additional items for the space. These included some modular seating, two beanbags, and a large rug; as well as smaller items such as shelf sitters, Perspex book stands and Perspex poster holders. All of these items were to make the whole space more attractive and to allow for promoting the books.

Adding the pupils to the Library Management System (LMS) was easily achieved using SIMS and it had been decided that children would be using cards rather than biometrics so that there was no requirement to take their fingerprints and the safeguarding implications that would bring.

The initial meeting with the staff was held on 19 March and they were brought up to date with the project. They were able to ask questions and to have a look at the finished space.

The library was ready for use by the end of March 2014 in line with the needs of the school; however there were complications over finishing Phase 2 of the project. During the whole process Bristol City Council had been undergoing a total staff review and at the end of 2013 they announced that the SLS would close at the end of March 2014. This gave us a second timescale to work to, as no staff would be available to work with the school after this date. There was an added issue due to redundancy terms which meant that staff could not work with Barton Hill on a consultancy basis either. The school itself was becoming focused on the transfer to Academy status, so that whilst it now had an attractive and modern library it was not able to take further steps to integrate the library into the life of the school. Two years on, in 2016, I am glad to say that the school is now working hard to fulfil the potential that they created in this project.

Appendix 1
Further Reading

■ Chartered Institute of Library and Information Professionals (2014. *The Primary School Library Guidelines*, London: CILIP.

Includes a section, 'Creating the environment' http://primaryschoollibraryguidelines.org.uk/

■ Dubber, G. (2016) *Beyond Beanbags: Designing Inspirational Secondary School Library Spaces*. Swindon: School Library Association.

Includes several detailed case studies.

■ Greenwood, Helen. Creaser, Claire. Maynard, Sally. (2008). *Successful Primary School Libraries: Case Studies of Good Practice*. London. Booktrust.

http://www.lboro.ac.uk/microsites/infosci/lisu/downloads/successful-prim-sch-libs.pdf

■ Harrison, K and Adams, T. (2007). *Practical Paperwork: Policy Making and Development Planning for the Primary School Library*. Swindon: School Library Association.

Includes several detailed case studies.

■ IFLA, School Libraries and Resource Centers Section (2nd ed. 2015), *IFLA/UNESCO School Library Guidelines*.

https://www.ifla.org/publications/node/36978

■ Loh Chin Ee (2015). 'Mapping Effective School Library Spaces' in *The School Librarian*, Volume 63, Number 2, Summer 2015

■ Elizabeth Lawrence and Frances Sinclair. 'Small But Perfectly Formed: A New Library for Stenness Community School' in *The School Librarian*, Volume 61, Number 1, Spring 2013

Appendix 2
Online Resources

■ Building Bulletin 103: Area Guidelines for Mainstream Schools

https://www.gov.uk/government/publications/mainstream-schools-area-guidelines

This guidance is aimed at school providers, local authorities, dioceses and building professionals. It will also assist school staff and governors involved in school building projects.

■ Baseline Designs for Schools

https://www.gov.uk/government/collections/school-building-design-and-maintenance

In this resource you will find information on baseline designs for schools. These demonstrate good practice that can be achieved within the set cost and area allowances. The details of the baseline designs are set out, together with associated drawings and technical analyses.

■ Designing Libraries

www.designinglibraries.org.uk

This is a resource for public library planning, design and building but could also be useful for schools. Its menu provides access to a list of useful publications and, via links, to suppliers of shelving, etc. A number of British suppliers, whose product range includes shelving and furniture for children and school libraries, are listed below.

■ Designed for Learning: School Libraries

YouTube: https://www.youtube.com/watch?v=3nKzEYPKG1U

A useful 2007 video from CILIP.

■ School Library Association (SLA)

www.sla.org.uk

This resource offers a wealth of information and support for school libraries with additional resources for SLA members.

■ CILIP (Chartered Institute of Library and Information Professionals)

http://primaryschoollibraryguidelines.org.uk/

This is an attractive and informative website for you to explore.

Appendix 3
Shelving, Furniture and Furnishing Suppliers

BGU Manufacturing Co.

(now part of Librex – see below)

BGU Manufacturing are specialists in the manufacture of library stationery and book protection materials. Also provide library shelving and furniture.

Cambridge Shelving Ltd
Unit 15, Lancaster Way Business Park
Ely
Cambridgeshire,
CB6 3NW
Contact: John Findlay
Telephone: 01353 665533
Web: http://www.reddisplays.com
Email: info@reddisplays.com

Cambridge Shelving Ltd purchased all the designs, website and all former RED and popular Remploy school library shelving ranges for continued production and supply direct to schools from their Cambridgeshire base at Ely.

DPC
Britannia Storage Systems Ltd
Lancaster Way, Earls Colne
Colchester
Essex
CO6 2NS
Tel: 01787 224411
Fax: 01787 223038
Web: http://www.britannia-storage.co.uk/
Email: Brians@brit-star.u-net.com

DPC Have been manufacturing and designing library furniture for over 20 years.

Fg Library
Concept House
Upton Valley Way East
Pineham Business Park
Northampton
NN4 9EF

Tel: 01604 755 954
Fax: 01604 586 980
Email: library@fggroup.co.uk
Web: www.fglibrary.co.uk/

Fg Library Products is a design led manufacturer of custom made library and general office furniture. Their website provides useful case studies of school library refurbishments

Gresswell
Freepost ANG0802
Hoddesdon
Herts
EN11 0BR
Tel: 01992 45 45 11
Email: orders@gresswell.com
Web: http://www.gresswell.co.uk/

Gresswells offer a wide choice in library supplies, furniture and display to assist you in the smooth running of your library and to help make your library environment an attractive and welcoming place for visitors.

Demco Worldwide Ltd
Demco Interiors
Shipton Way
Express Park
Rushden
Northamptonshire
NN10 6GL
Tel: 01992 454600
Fax: 01933 318918
Email: enquiries@demcointeriors.co.uk
Website: http://www.demcointeriors.co.uk/

Demco Interiors are one of the UK's leading library design consultancy, specialising in the design, specification, installation and project management of library refurbishment and new build projects.

Finnmade Furniture Solutions Ltd.
6 Newlands Lane
Hitchin
SG4 9AY
Hertfordshire
Tel: 01462 452001
Fax: 01462 452002
Web: http://www.finnmade.co.uk/

Finnmade Furniture Solutions specialize in the supply and installation of shelving, furniture and accessories for school, public and business libraries.

Librex
Colwick Road
Nottingham
NG2 4BG
Tel: 0115 950 4664/0115 958 0032
Fax: 0800 132295 (free fax)

Email:sales@librex.co.uk
Web: http://www.librex.co.uk/

Librex have been an established library supplier for almost 40 years. A comprehensive selection of goods is offered including: Library furniture; Charging equipment; Display equipment

Opening the Book
Opening the Book Promotions
7b St Michael's Court
Warstone Parade East
Jewellery Quarter
Birmingham
B18 6NR
Tel: 0121 246 8260
Fax: 0121 246 3197
Email: anya@openingthebook.com
Web: http://www.openingthebook.com/

Opening the Book have designed and installed more than 50 libraries of all sizes and types. Their website also has some very useful photographic examples of libraries they have designed, including primary and secondary school libraries.

Peters Bookselling Services
The Kit Shop
120 Bromsgrove St,
Birmingham, B5 6RJ
Tel: 0121 666 6646
Fax: 0121 666 7033
Email: sales@peters-books.co.uk
Web: http://www.peters-books.co.uk/

Peters are the largest independent library supplier in the country. They have a new showroom featuring all of the products from their current range of library furniture including shelving, display units and a colourful selection of rugs.

Ryco Book Protection Svs Ltd
Unit 10 Ballywaltrim Business Center
Bray
Co. Wicklow
Ireland
Tel: 00353 (0) 1 2867055
Fax: 00353 (0) 1 2867095

Freephone in the UK: 0800 783 5156
Ryco offer a range of high quality, library standard book covering materials and supply to many libraries.

Serota Library Furniture
SEROTA Ltd
92 Hilliard Road
Northwood, Middlesex
HA6 1SW
Email: info@serota.co.uk
Web: http://www.serota.co.uk/

The Serota family has over 100 years' experience of furniture manufacturing and fitting. All the furniture is custom-made so you choose a solution that suits your space.

Zioxi
57 High St.
Tetsworth
Oxfordshire
OX9 7BS
Tel: 01844 280 123
Website: https://zioxi.co.uk/

Also available from the SLA

Cultivating Curiosity: Information Literacy Skills and the Primary School Library

by Geoff Dubber and Sarah Pavey

978-1-911222-15-6   £13.50 (SLA members £9.00)

Cultivating curiosity in children in primary schools is one of the most important things that we can do for them. Developing an enthusiasm for learning is at the very heart of human development and a central reason for teaching information and digital literacy, and is a crucial focus for school library work. This new edition includes information about the most recent primary curriculum, government initiatives and recent inspection changes in respect of the school library and digital media. It explains the importance of embedding information literacy into a whole school and curriculum context, making use of modern technology where appropriate. It outlines and explains the processes of research for young children and shows ways that teachers and librarians can develop and promote information and digital literacy through the primary school library and link it to classroom practice. It also includes a very useful and practical case study, some templates and a reading list.

A World of Books in Translation

by Joy Court and Daniel Hahn

978-1-911222-00-2   £13.50 (SLA members £9.00)

'Books in translation help us all to reach beyond our own language and culture,' writes David Almond, yet until recently few foreign children's books were translated into English. In this Riveting Reads publication our two renowned editors, Joy Court and Daniel Hahn, go some way to illuminate the wealth of material now coming from all corners of the world. They provide a superb selection of book reviews for the Under 8s through to the 14+ age ranges – titles that really should be on our library shelves. With pithy and illuminating annotations covering a wealth of topics and genres, *A World of Books in Translation* is an excellent guide that reflects the 90% of the world that does not speak English as its first language.

Budgeting for Success: Planning and Managing the Primary School Library Finances

by Karen Horsfield and Susan Staniforth

978-1-911222-08-8   £13.50 (SLA members £9.00)

We all know budgets are tight. Planning and then managing the finances of the primary school library, whether large or small, is an essential job for all primary library coordinators. Planning ahead, knowing and outlining the budget that you need to be effective and having a clear understanding of the library's annual budget cycle are all important aspects of budget success. Here is our revised and updated Guideline that includes clear advice and useful templates to help you through this important process. It also includes two new case studies on this important aspect of work.